Rebecca Targett Productions
in association with Raising Silv
present

Now This Is Not The End

by Rose Lewenstein

arcola
theatre

Now This Is Not The End was first performed at the
Arcola Theatre, London, on 3 June 2015

Now This Is Not The End
by Rose Lewenstein

CAST (in order of appearance)
Rosie	Jasmine Blackborow
Sebastian	Daniel Donskoy
Eva	Brigit Forsyth
Susan	Wendy Nottingham
Paul	Andrew Whipp
Arnold	Bernard Lloyd

CREATIVE TEAM
Director	Katie Lewis
Designer	Holly Pigott
Sound Designer/Composer	Dan Jeffries
Lighting Designer	Prema Mehta
Dialect Coach	Luke Nicholson
Design Assistant	Anna Kezia Williams
Creative Associate	John Manning

PRODUCTION TEAM
Producer	Rebecca Targett
Associate Producer	Raising Silver Theatre
Stage Manager	Amy McLean
Production Manager	Jamie Kluckers
Marketing	Jo Hutchison International
Press Representation	Kate Morley PR

Biographies

Jasmine Blackborow | Rosie
Trained at RCSSD.

Theatre credits include: *Dracula* (New Vic); *As You Like It, Enemies, The Seagull* (Royal Central School of Speech and Drama); *All or Nothing* (Edinburgh Fringe); *Macbeth, Henry V* (University of East Anglia); and *stoning mary* (Norwich Puppet Theatre).

Daniel Donskoy | Sebastian
Theatre credits include: *Bad Jews* (Theatre Royal Bath/Arts Theatre); *Soviet Zion* (The Lost Theatre); *Porn Virgins* (Phoenix Arts Club) and *The Apple Tree* (Rose and Crown).

Film credits include: *The Honourable Rebel* (dir Mike Fraser); *Fatal Romantics* (dir Resul Keech) and *Prometheus Rising* (dir Diana Fröse).

Brigit Forsyth | Eva
Theatre credits include: *People* (National Theatre tour); *The Missing* (National Theatre of Scotland); *Calendar Girls* (Noël Coward/national tour); *Carrie's War* (national tour); *Noises Off* (Birmingham REP); *The Triumph of Love, The Importance of Being Earnest* (Royal Exchange, Manchester); *Humble Boy* (national tour) and *Hamlet* (West Yorkshire Playhouse).

Telveision credits include: Thelma from *Whatever Happened to the Likely Lads* and *Still Open All Hours, Playing the Field, Tom, Dick and Harriet, The Practice, Sharon and Elsie, Waterloo Road, Down to Earth, The Eustace Bros.* and *Nice Town.*

Film credits include: *Whatever Happened to the Likely Lads, Fanny and Elvis.*

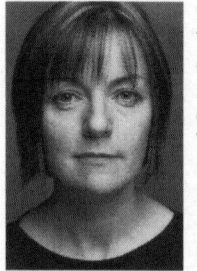

Wendy Nottingham | Susan

Theatre credits include: *Forgotten Voices* (Pleasance, Edinburgh); *Donkey Heart* (Old Red Lion); *The Winslow Boy* (Old Vic); *In Basildon* (Royal Court) and *Grief* (National Theatre). Television credits include: *Mr Selfridge, The Borgias, A Young Doctor's Notebook, Crimson Petal and the White, Getting On, Kingdom* and *Housewife 49*.

Film credits include: *Madame Bovary, Pudsey, Atonement, Notes on a Scandal, Babel, Vera Drake, Topsy-Turvy* and *Secrets and Lies*.

Andrew Whipp | Paul

Theatre credits include: *Farragut North* (Southwark Playhouse); *Dark at the Top of the Stairs* (Belgrade Coventry); *Macbeth, King Lear* (Shakespeare's Globe); *Arcadia, Celebration* (Gate, Dublin); *Much Ado About Nothing* (Stafford); *The Misanthrope* (Theatre Royal Bury St Edmunds); *Les Liaisons Dangereuses* (No.1 tour); *The Nerd* (No. 1 tour); *The Child* (Gate, Notting Hill); *King Lear, The Taming of the Shrew* (Ludlow Festival); *See How They Run* (Watermill); *The Invisible Man* (national tour).

Television credits include: *The Coroner, A Song for Jenny, Suspicion, Outlander, Spotless, Critical, Not Going Out, Holby City, When Harvey Met Bob, EastEnders; Bedlam, Doctors, City Lights, Love Lies Bleeding, Emmerdale, Absolute Power, Judge John Deed, Falling Apart, The New Professionals*.

Film includes: *Artificio Conceal, Silent Hours, The Fourth Kind, Amazing Grace*.

Bernard Lloyd | Arnold

Theatre credits include: *The Last Confession* (Chichester Festival Theatre/Theatre Royal Haymarket/international tour); *Pravda* (Birmingham REP); *Nicholas Nickleby, King Lear* (West Yorkshire Playhouse); *Imagine This* (New London); *Le Cid* (National Theatre); as well as extensive work for the RSC.

Television credits include: *Lewis, Trial and Retribution, A Christmas Carol, Pavements of Gold, Food for Ravens, A Dangerous Man, The Man from Pru* and *Under Milk Wood*.

Rose Lewenstein | Writer
Rose's first play *Ain't No Law Against Fish 'n' Chips* received a staged reading at the Royal Court Young Writers Festival 2012. Other theatre includes: *Game of Life* (The Yard); *Only Human* (Theatre503) and *Entries on Love* (Rich Mix). Rose developed *Now This Is Not The End* on the Royal Court's Supergroup.

Katie Lewis | Director
Katie Lewis trained as a theatre director at Birkbeck College, after reading Philosophy at the University of Sussex. She founded Raising Silver Theatre, a company committed to creating opportunities for female practitioners and producing work from the most exciting female playwrights. Katie has been Resident Director for the National Theatre's UK and Ireland tour of *One Man Two Guvnors* and Assistant Director for the Royal Shakespeare Company's 2013 ensemble working on *As You Like It* and *A Midsummer Night's Dream*.

Directing includes *The Rover* (RSC Studio); *Daisy Pulls It Off* (ALRA); *The Firewatchers*, which was nominated for two Off-West Awards (Old Red Lion); *A Pocket Full of Dreams - A Tennessee Williams Collection* (ALRA); *Red Riding Hood and The Wolves* (Edinburgh Festival); *Unmanned* (Miniaturists, Arcola); *The Jewish Wife, Mr Happiness* (Manchester Library Theatre); *Eight* (Lowry Studio); *Kitty Gulliver* (Write on the Edge Festival, Brian Friel Theatre, Belfast); *Fractures, The Mixer* (Slice, Theatre503); *Spoonface Steinberg* (King's Head/Etcetera)

Holly Pigott | Designer
Holly graduated from the Royal Welsh College of Music and Drama with a First Class Honours in Theatre and Performance Design. In 2011 she was shortlisted as one of twelve finalists in the Linbury Prize for Stage Design and she has since spent a year as a Trainee Designer with the Royal Shakespeare Company. Design credits include: *La Scala Di Seta* (Linbury Studio, ROH); *The Island* (Young Vic/JMK Award); *Klippies, East of Berlin* (Southwark Playhouse); *The Prophet* (Gate); *Sex With A Stranger* (Trafalgar Studios); *Elegy for a Lady* and *The Yalta Game* (Salisbury Playhouse); *Fleabag* (Underbell/Soho/UK tour); *Lean* (Tristan Bates); *Now This Is Not The End, Façade, Eight Songs For a Mad King, Handel Furioso* and *Sound of a Voice* (Arcola); *Die Fledermaus* (King's Head/OperaUpClose); *Below the Belt* (Pleasance Courtyard/Omnibus Theatre); *The Cage Birds* (LAMDA's Linbury Studio) and *Who's Afraid of Rachel Roberts* (Torch Theatre).

Dan Jeffries | Sound Designer/Composer
Dan Jeffries' music has been performed around the world, notably in London (Barbican Centre), Newcastle (Sage Gateshead), New York (Dixon Place) and Copenhagen (DKDM). Theatre work includes *The Importance of Being Earnest* (Theatre Royal Haymarket); *The Domino Heart* (Finborough); *Mucky Kid* (Theatre503);*The Hothouse* (Oxford Playhouse) and *The Firewatchers* (Old Red Lion) for which he was nominated for an Off West End award. In film and television Dan has written additional music for shows such as *Silent Witness* (BBC) and *DCI Banks* (Leftbank/ITV) assisting Sheridan Tongue, and in 2013-14 scored two short films by Alexander Darby: *The Wishing Horse* and *Catkins*. Dan also works as an engineer and producer in the UK and abroad.

Prema Mehta | Lighting Designer
Prema graduated from the Guildhall School of Music and Drama. She has designed the lighting for over one hundred drama and dance productions, including: *Jefferson's Garden* (Watford Palace Theatre); *Hercules* (New Art Club on tour); *Bells* (part of the Mayor of London's outdoor festival, Showtime); *The Great Extension* (Theatre Royal Stratford East); *Calcutta Kosher* (Arcola); *The Electric Hills* (Liverpool Everyman); *Dhamaka* (O2 Arena) and *Maaya* (Westminster Hall). Prema recently designed for Madame Tussauds London, working on the launch of a new A-List party figure. Further details are available at www.premamehta.com

Luke Nicholson | Dialect Coach
Luke is a freelance dialect coach based in London, who has taught students from fifty different countries. He is a member of the US-based DialectCoaches.com network, the Voice and Speech Trainers Association, and the International Phonetic Association. He holds a first-class degree in German and Italian from the University of Birmingham, and the International Phonetic Association Certificate from University College London. Additionally, he has trained as an actor at East 15 and as a dialect coach with Knight-Thompson Speechwork in New York. As well as coaching actors, Luke helps non-native English speakers sound English through his company ImproveYourAccent.co.uk

Amy McLean | Stage Manager
Amy attended the Royal Welsh College of Music and Drama to study an MA in Theatre and Event Management. Her theatre work includes a series of projects with Islington Community Theatre including *Other (Please Specify)*, *Atoms* and *Brainstorm* which is being revived in July at the National Theatre; *Sister Act* (Kilworth House Theatre); *Orlando Paladino* (PurPur Opera, International Tour); *Parsifal* (Royal Opera House); *MicroMEGAS* (Shadow Opera);

The Future For Beginners (LIVEARTSHOW); *Dido and Aeneas* and *Britten's Women* (Bath International Music Festival); *Flight* (Sherman Cymru) and *Crazy in Love* (Upstairs At The Gatehouse).

Jamie Kluckers | Production Manager
Jamie trained in Production at Guildford School of Acting and has since worked in the industry as Production Manager, Technical Manager and Stage Manager. In 2013, Jamie set up JKP Technical Production Services and has been supplying technical production support for a variety of clients including The National Trust as well as various universities, private schools and colleges. His most recent theatre credits include *Legally Blonde, Twang!* (GSA); *Guys and Dolls, Gypsy* (Chichester Festival Theatre); and *WINK* (Theatre503).

Rebecca Targett | Producer
Rebecca is an independent producer. Productions include: *Spokesong, The Flouers O'Edinburgh, The Wallace, Little Red Hen, Jock: Scotland on Trial* (Finborough); *In Loving Memory* (Birmingham REP/mac Birmingham); *Ordinary Days* (Rosemary Branch); *Three to Four Days* (Theatre503/Surgeon's Hall The Spaces, Edinburgh Fringe); the world's first stage adaptation of Studio Ghibli's *Princess Mononoke* for Whole Hog Theatre which received sell-out runs at New Diorama Theatre before transferring to The AiiATheater, Japan.

Rebecca currently works at Told by an Idiot and has previously worked at Jamie Wilson Productions, Royal & Derngate, Northampton (supported by the Stage One Apprentice Scheme) and Birmingham Repertory Theatre. She has previous experience at the Royal Shakespeare Company, Sonia Friedman Productions, Ambassador's Theatre Group and Salisbury Playhouse. She was the winner of the Edinburgh Festival Fringe Emerging Producer's Programme 2013 and was mentored by Tony Reekie, Imaginate. Rebecca is mentored by Sarah Ellis, Digital Producer at the Royal Shakespeare Company. Rebecca was also awarded the Stage One Bursary in 2013 and is mentored by Nicola Seed and Martin Sutherland.

Raising Silver Theatre | Associate Producer
Raising Silver Theatre was set up in 2011. The company is committed to promoting opportunities for female practitioners and gender parity in its casting. Raising Silver develops and revives work from the most exciting female playwrights. The company's inaugural production, *The Firewatchers* by Laura Stevens, was nominated for two Off West End awards. In 2014 Raising Silver carried out research and development workshops on Aphra Behn's *The Rover* in the RSC Studio. The company has a growing education strand, delivering a range of workshops across the country. www.raisingsilvertheatre.co.uk

PRODUCTION ACKNOWLEDGEMENTS

David Ferrier, Make Believe Arts, Sue Lloyd, Sabrina Jantuah, Alzheimer's Society, Migration Museum, Sue McAlphine, Astrid Kohler, Silke Arnold-de Simine, Nicola Seed, Kate Sketchley, Melissa Rosenbaum, The Wiener Library and Sue Bermange.

SUPPORTED BY

Stage One, Arts Council England, The Royal Victoria Hall Foundation, Unity Theatre Trust, Second Generation Network, Imperial War Museum and Holocaust Education Trust.

Arcola Theatre is one of London's leading off-West End theatres.

Locally engaged and internationally minded, Arcola stages a diverse programme of plays, operas and musicals. World-class productions from major artists appear alongside cutting-edge work from the most exciting emerging companies.

Arcola delivers one of London's most extensive community engagement programmes, creating over 5000 opportunities every year. By providing research and development space to diverse artists, Arcola champions theatre that's more engaging and representative. Its pioneering environmental initiatives are internationally renowned, and aim to make Arcola the world's first carbon-neutral theatre.

Artistic Director
Mehmet Ergen

Executive Producer
Leyla Nazli

Executive Director
Ben Todd

Creative Engagement Manager
Nick Connaughton

Sustainability Manager
Feimatta Conteh

IT Manager
Nick Cripps

Front of House & Box Office Manager
Charlotte Croft

Marketing Manager
Jack Gamble

Business Development Manager
Richard Kemp-Harper

Technical Manager
Geoff Hense

Bar Manager
Jonny Powell

Operations Manager
Laura Rolinson

Facilities Manager
David Todd

Assistant Bar Manager
Patrick Duncombe

Assistant Front of House & Box Office Manager
Miriam Mahony

Duty Managers and Box Office
James Morris
Mary Roubos
Lottie Vallis

Bar Supervisors
Oya Bacak
Joe Cochrane

With grateful thanks to our ushers, interns, volunteers and those on work placements, and to our Supporters, Patrons and other donors.

ARTS COUNCIL ENGLAND · Esmée Fairbairn · J PAUL GETTY JNR CHARITABLE TRUST · Bloomberg · Hackney

---

www.arcolatheatre.com   020 7503 1646   24 Ashwin Street, Dalston, London E8 3DL

NOW THIS IS NOT THE END

Rose Lewenstein

Acknowledgements

Leo Butler and everyone on the Royal Court Supergroup,
Leyla Nazli and everyone at the Arcola, Harriet Pennington Legh,
Rebecca Targett, Wolfram Kosch, Astrid Kohler, Luke Nicholson,
Andie Lewenstein, Leonie Mellinger and Katie Lewis.

R.L.

Characters

EVA, *seventies to eighties, British, of German-Jewish descent*
SUSAN, *forties to fifties, Eva's daughter*
ROSIE, *eighteen to twenty-two, Susan's daughter*
ARNOLD, *eighties, British, of German-Jewish descent,*
    Eva's husband
PAUL, *fifties, British, Susan's partner*
SEBASTIAN, *late twenties, German, Rosie's boyfriend*

Notes

A line with no full stop at the end of it means the character is interrupted

New lines and spaces within a speech indicate the flow of the speech

(…) at the end of a line means the speech trails off

(…) on its own means the character either chooses not to speak or doesn't know what to say

This text went to press before the end of rehearsals and so may differ slightly from the play as performed.

One

2014

Darkness. An answerphone beep.

EVA (*voice-over*). Rosie?

Rosie are you there?

Rosie I can't remember when it's your birthday. Is it soon? What would you like? Will you buy yourself something from me? Buy yourself something from me and I'll write you a cheque when I see you.

Rosie?

When will I see you?

I want to know what it is you would like for your birthday. Is it Easter soon or Christmas?

No, it's Easter. There's a man who comes to dig up the flowers. I told him to leave them alone but he said he's helping them or something. I told him it's too late. They'll all be dead in ten years.

Is it Easter soon or Christmas? What would you like? Will you buy yourself something from me and I'll write you a cheque?

Well. Why shouldn't I have Christmas if I want to.

Click as the phone hangs up.

Silence.

Lights up on a loft apartment in Kreuzberg, Berlin. Messy but minimalist.

ROSIE *and* SEBASTIAN *stand either side of an open suitcase.* ROSIE *is packing throughout.*

ROSIE. I don't know.

SEBASTIAN. Gut feeling though.

ROSIE. Is that I don't know.

SEBASTIAN. Guts don't say things like 'don't know'.

ROSIE. Mine does.

SEBASTIAN. You must have a sense. A feeling. One way or the other.

ROSIE. It isn't something I can pin down.

SEBASTIAN. Because you say you're going home but

ROSIE. Yes, home, London.

SEBASTIAN. and the reason I'm asking is because

ROSIE. What else am I supposed to say?

SEBASTIAN. well in German the word holds a different meaning.

ROSIE. I know what it means.

SEBASTIAN. It's untranslatable.

ROSIE. It's patriotic.

SEBASTIAN. No, more than that. Something much deeper. A deep visceral connection.

ROSIE. …

Well I don't have it.

SEBASTIAN. Everyone has it.

ROSIE. I don't feel it.

SEBASTIAN. It's what makes us people.

ROSIE. Then maybe I'm not a person.

SEBASTIAN. Will you stop that.

ROSIE. I told Mum and Paul I'd be packed. I told them there'd be *Kaffee und Kuchen*.

SEBASTIAN. Will you stop that and listen.

ROSIE. And you know what my mother is like, I mean for fuck's sake she can hardly make a cup of tea without putting it on her to-do list.

SEBASTIAN. You're not listening to me.

ROSIE. Their whole trip has been organised around me flying back with them tomorrow.

SEBASTIAN. Not even engaging with what I'm

ROSIE. Breakfast at the top of the Reichstag, then coffee and cake, then a taxi to the airport.

The packing becomes more urgent.

SEBASTIAN. Rosie.

ROSIE. A taxi to the airport to catch a plane to take us *home*.

SEBASTIAN. Rosie no one is making you leave, okay? No one is forcing you, in fact it's the opposite.

And I wouldn't ask, I wouldn't even bring it up if I thought for one minute that you going back to London was what you really wanted, what you really felt in your heart and in your gut and will you LEAVE THE FUCKING SUITCASE ALONE.

ROSIE *stops*.

ROSIE. Please, Sebastian. Don't make this any harder.

SEBASTIAN. I'm only asking.

ROSIE. You're asking me abstract questions.

SEBASTIAN. I'm just trying to work out

ROSIE. Abstract questions about the meanings of words.

SEBASTIAN. I'm trying to work out what you want, because phone calls and emails and Skype sex

ROSIE. Skype sex?

SEBASTIAN. well that's not what I want.

ROSIE. I don't want Skype sex either.

SEBASTIAN. But that's the point, there won't be any sex, there won't be any physical contact at all

and I'm not saying that sex is the important thing here because it's not, I mean it is *a* point, but it's not *the* point

What I'm saying, what I am saying is that I

ROSIE. Don't.

SEBASTIAN. Okay.

But I want you to stay.

Here. With me.

ROSIE. …

SEBASTIAN. You have a choice.

ROSIE. I know.

SEBASTIAN. 'But.'

ROSIE. But this was always the plan.

SEBASTIAN. But you have options.

ROSIE. This was always going to happen.

SEBASTIAN. You could do your final year here, that's an option.

ROSIE. It's not as simple as that. I need to focus.

SEBASTIAN. What, you can't focus here?

ROSIE. I've got a lot of catching up to do if I want to get a two-one.

SEBASTIAN. Right.

ROSIE. And I know it's hard. Fuck it's really fucking hard, but we knew this from the start.

SEBASTIAN. Okay we knew this but still, it's excuses, you're convincing yourself.

ROSIE. No, I'm

SEBASTIAN. Lying to yourself and

ROSIE. I'm being realistic.

SEBASTIAN. and you're just dismissing it. Dismissing the whole idea because it wasn't part of your plan.

ROSIE. Look.

SEBASTIAN. ...

ROSIE. I've done nothing this year, I

SEBASTIAN. This is nothing?

ROSIE. No I don't mean

SEBASTIAN. Me and you is nothing?

ROSIE. I meant studying.

SEBASTIAN. Okay but you've learnt German.

ROSIE. Well that's kind of a given.

SEBASTIAN. And you're good at it.

ROSIE. Doesn't mean I can write about it.

SEBASTIAN. You have an ear for it.

ROSIE. Well yeah but

SEBASTIAN. And like that's obvious, of course you do

ROSIE. but you're good at English too.

I'm not saying...

I'm just saying.

Silence.

SEBASTIAN. You know I can't come with you.

ROSIE. I never asked you to.

SEBASTIAN. I couldn't live in London.

ROSIE. Wouldn't dream of asking you.

SEBASTIAN. Couldn't live in a shoebox.

ROSIE. What?

SEBASTIAN. That and I can only make the work I make here.

ROSIE. I know.

SEBASTIAN. It's specific to

ROSIE. Berlin, I know, I'm just

> I'm just putting it out there because it seems like your reasoning for all this is based on some, I dunno, some abstract concept of where you or I belong and it's

> well it's priorities, isn't it, and I can't help thinking, feeling, that *your* thinking is influenced by

> by your work, whereas mine is

SEBASTIAN. ...

> I am spilling my heart out to you here.

ROSIE. Pouring.

SEBASTIAN. What?

ROSIE. Spilling's for guts.

SEBASTIAN. Are you

ROSIE. Never mind.

SEBASTIAN. Are you correcting my English?

ROSIE. Look it doesn't matter.

SEBASTIAN. Is this really the time to be correcting my fucking English?

ROSIE. No, I'm sorry, go on.

SEBASTIAN. It's different for me.

> It is. I've been working hard for this.

ROSIE. I know you have.

SEBASTIAN. I am getting *paid* to make art. Do you know how rare that is? Do you have any idea how unheard of it is to get *money* for ideas that are in your head?

ROSIE. Yeah I know that, Sebastian, I'm not questioning that, I think it's amazing, I think *you* are amazing

SEBASTIAN. Opportunities like this don't just come out of nowhere.

ROSIE. but you see in saying that, like what you're implying with that

SEBASTIAN. All I'm saying is that I need to be here.

ROSIE. Right. Yeah.

SEBASTIAN. Because. It is different for me. Things are starting to take off.

ROSIE. But me I can study anywhere.

SEBASTIAN. Not anywhere. Here.

ROSIE. I'm transportable.

SEBASTIAN. Your degree is in *German*.

ROSIE. The girlfriend equivalent of a fucking caravan.

SEBASTIAN. What?

ROSIE. You're basically calling me a caravan.

SEBASTIAN. Okay. I give up.

ROSIE. You give up.

SEBASTIAN. I'm not going to beg.

ROSIE. No. Good.

ROSIE *continues to pack in silence.*

SEBASTIAN. So.

This is it then.

No answer.

She picks up a fur jacket.

ROSIE. Forgot I had this.

Holds it to her face.

SEBASTIAN. Is this?

It?

It's like she can't hear him.

ROSIE. She called again today.

Tries the jacket on.

I've stopped picking up.

Shit of me, isn't it.

Selfish.

SEBASTIAN. ...

So what's next.

ROSIE. Huh?

SEBASTIAN. What happens. Once you're back in London, once you've graduated with a two-one in the German language. What's the plan.

ROSIE. I don't know.

SEBASTIAN. Surely you must have a plan.

ROSIE. I DON'T KNOW.

SEBASTIAN. Fuck Rosie, is there anything you *do* know?

ROSIE. I thought I'd figure that out this year. I thought I'd figure out a lot of things on my year abroad but…

SEBASTIAN. But what.

ROSIE. I fell in love, didn't I.

Silence.

And that definitely wasn't part of the plan. And whatever the plan is now I'm supposed to stick to it because that's what I do because that's the kind of person I am, okay? The kind of person who sticks to a plan.

SEBASTIAN. Okay.

ROSIE. I need a plan.

SEBASTIAN. I get it.

ROSIE. Otherwise I'm

Lost.

SEBASTIAN. But you couldn't answer the question.

ROSIE. Because yes. The word. *Heimat*. It *is* untranslatable. But that's nothing to do with language. It's untranslatable to

It doesn't apply

It's never applied

to people like me.

SEBASTIAN. Gut feeling I said.

ROSIE. Isn't geographical.

SEBASTIAN. But even if it isn't a place.

ROSIE. If it's a person.

SEBASTIAN. Yeah.

ROSIE. Then yeah. You're my person.

They stare at each other for a moment.

SEBASTIAN. So you'll

I mean

Does this mean

Are you saying

…

ROSIE *looks out the window.*

Rosie?

Silence.

ROSIE. I want to get curtains.

SEBASTIAN. …

ROSIE. I don't like the sun telling me when I have to wake up.

SEBASTIAN. Okay.

ROSIE. And a heater.

SEBASTIAN. I'll get a heater.

ROSIE. I want it to be comfortable.

SEBASTIAN. I love you, Rosie.

ROSIE. Yeah.

SEBASTIAN. And you love me.

ROSIE. Yes. I do.

He's still staring at her.

What?

SEBASTIAN. No. I don't know.

ROSIE. You don't know?

SEBASTIAN. I mean I do. I do know.

ROSIE. Okay. Good.

Silence.

SEBASTIAN. Is it real?

ROSIE. What?

SEBASTIAN. The jacket.

ROSIE. It's vintage.

SEBASTIAN. Suits you.

ROSIE. Yeah.

Yeah I know.

Blackout.

Two

2011

The attic of a North London town house. Cluttered with boxes overspilling books, tapes, stuff...

ROSIE *sits on the floor, looking through boxes, flicking through books.* EVA, SUSAN *and* PAUL *stand amid the mess.*

EVA. We're throwing it all out.

SUSAN. All of it?

EVA. Yes, take what you like.

PAUL. Thanks, but we don't need any more books.

ROSIE. Nobody *needs* books.

PAUL. Don't need any more stuff.

EVA. It's smaller you see.

SUSAN. I only want the tape.

EVA. We've got hundreds of tapes.

SUSAN. But I only want this one.

   EVA *looks in one of the boxes.*

EVA. Mozart? Wagner?

PAUL. No, really, thanks.

EVA. We're throwing it all out.

   PAUL *finds a stool and settles down with a newspaper.*

SUSAN. Why now?

EVA. Because it's smaller. Do you want any, Rosie? Tapes?

ROSIE. I don't have a cassette player.

SUSAN. I mean I thought you liked it here.

EVA. Do you need one? We've got one somewhere.

ROSIE. Nobody listens to tapes any more.

SUSAN. Mum.

EVA. What?

SUSAN. I thought you liked it here.

EVA. It's too big.

SUSAN. Is that what Arnold says?

EVA. He doesn't like the stairs.

SUSAN. Even so.

EVA. Arnold's terribly ill.

SUSAN. Since when?

EVA. He's practically a cripple.

SUSAN. Oh don't be silly, he just eats too much.

EVA. It's his heart.

SUSAN. Well moving house won't help.

EVA. There's a lift you see.

SUSAN. Moving house is a big upheaval.

EVA. In the new what's-it-called, there's a lift.

SUSAN. A huge upheaval, isn't it, Paul.

PAUL. Hmm?

SUSAN. I mean at your age.

EVA. What's wrong with my age?

SUSAN. Nothing's wrong with it.

EVA. I can touch my toes, look.

SUSAN. Yes you've shown me before.

EVA. Look Rosie, I can touch my toes.

ROSIE. Yeah, that's really cool.

EVA. Can you, Susan? Touch your toes?

SUSAN. I don't know, Mum.

EVA. Try it.

SUSAN. I don't want to try it.

ROSIE. Go on, Mum.

PAUL. Rosie.

EVA. Would you believe it I can touch my toes.

I don't feel it. Old.

SUSAN. No, well, good.

EVA. I see them in the street. Old people. You know, the doddery ones. I'm not like them at all.

SUSAN. No.

EVA. Am I.

ROSIE. No, Grandma.

ROSIE *smiles*.

EVA. Haven't you got lovely teeth.

ROSIE. Thanks.

EVA. Hasn't she got lovely teeth, Susan.

SUSAN. Yes I suppose.

EVA. Show me yours.

SUSAN. I'm not a horse.

EVA. Not as white as Rosie's.

SUSAN. I expect they were when I was eighteen.

EVA. Lovely teeth.

SUSAN. And if she keeps smoking like she does then they won't stay white for long.

ROSIE. Bleaching kits, Mum.

EVA. Shall I make some tea?

PAUL. Tea would be nice.

EVA. Rosie will you have some *Lebkuchen*?

ROSIE. No thanks.

EVA. Marzipan?

ROSIE. We just had lunch.

EVA. Not even a piece of chocolate?

SUSAN. She's not hungry.

EVA. Are you slimming?

ROSIE. No.

EVA. You're ever so slim.

SUSAN. She doesn't want anything.

EVA. We're throwing it all out.

SUSAN. To eat I mean.

EVA. All this stuff.

PAUL. Don't need any more stuff.

EVA. So take what you'd like.

SUSAN. You know what I'd like.

EVA. …

   I'd better get Arnold.

SUSAN. I shouldn't need to ask Arnold's permission.

EVA. He's digging up the flowers.

SUSAN. Then leave him to it.

EVA. He got in a fight with one of the neighbours.

SUSAN. A fight?

EVA. Or something.

SUSAN. A physical fight?

EVA. I can't remember.

SUSAN. The neighbours who grow tomatoes?

EVA. What?

SUSAN. You told me your next-door neighbours grew tomatoes.

EVA. Did I?

SUSAN. Yes. You said that Arnold made a bolognese with the tomatoes from the neighbours next door.

EVA shakes her head in bemusement.

EVA. They still don't get it.

SUSAN. Don't get what?

EVA. You know.

SUSAN. Do I?

EVA. We confuse them.

SUSAN. Oh. Well it's complicated.

EVA. It's not.

SUSAN. To some people.

ROSIE. What's complicated?

PAUL. Families.

SUSAN. Is that why he wants to move?

EVA. We're moving because of the stairs.

Silence.

Who wants tea?

PAUL. Yes please.

SUSAN. Rosie, tell your grandmother about the course.

ROSIE. Oh right, yeah, I got into UCL.

EVA. Aren't you clever.

SUSAN. She's decided to study German.

EVA. How marvellous.

ROSIE. Yeah. So I get to spend a year abroad.

SUSAN. She can't wait to get away from us.

ROSIE. Berlin.

EVA. I lived in Berlin you know.

ROSIE. I know.

EVA. *Essener Straße*.

ROSIE. Where's that then?

EVA. The house with the blue door.

ROSIE. Right.

EVA. Except that it isn't blue any more.

ROSIE. …

EVA. You could see the park from my bedroom window.

ROSIE. The Tear Garden?

EVA. *Tiergarten*.

SUSAN. You talked about that house. On the tape.

EVA. What?

SUSAN. D'you suppose it'll be in one of these boxes?

EVA. I'd better get Arnold.

SUSAN. If he doesn't want to say hello…

EVA. He knows where everything is.

SUSAN. But he wasn't even there when we

EVA. Hold on.

SUSAN. Mum.

   EVA *exits*.

   Well?

PAUL. Hmm?

SUSAN. What d'you think?

PAUL. I dunno. Seems her usual self.

SUSAN. She doesn't. Couldn't even remember the tomatoes.

PAUL. Well. She does that sometimes.

SUSAN. Does what?

PAUL. Pretends.

SUSAN. Why would she pretend about something like that?

PAUL. I don't know.

SUSAN. No but in your professional opinion.

PAUL. I'm not a doctor.

SUSAN. I mean if you were psychoanalysing her.

PAUL. But I'm not.

SUSAN. But if you were.

PAUL. You know what I think.

SUSAN. …

PAUL. She's manipulative.

ROSIE. She's not.

PAUL. How hard is it to make a pot of tea?

SUSAN. She remembers the blue door but she can't remember the tomatoes…

ROSIE. They're different kinds of memories. One's long-term and one's

SUSAN. Well I think she should go for tests.

PAUL. Between them they're all right. What with his head and her heart.

SUSAN. Yes I don't think that's how it works, Paul.

PAUL. No I know, it was a joke.

SUSAN. 'Practically a cripple.' Honestly.

ROSIE. Wish he *would* have a heart attack, put us all out our misery.

SUSAN. Rosie.

ROSIE. Wouldn't you?

SUSAN. Yes but still.

PAUL. Well he's certainly doing his best to get rid of their assets.

SUSAN. How much d'you think it's going for. The house.

PAUL. No idea.

SUSAN. But roughly.

PAUL. In my 'professional opinion' I'd say roughly a lot.

ROSIE. Is that what you're worried about? The house?

SUSAN. No Rosie, I am worried about my mother.

ROSIE. But you don't think they'll leave you anything?

SUSAN. Oh don't be so crude.

ROSIE. But you think Arnold's gonna be a dick about it?

SUSAN. What's the matter with you?

ROSIE. Paul's the one who said it.

PAUL. I didn't say *that*.

SUSAN. You're hungover, aren't you.

ROSIE. No.

SUSAN. You know it's not compulsory to drink every single weekend.

ROSIE. I am not 'hungover'.

SUSAN. Or stay up all night.

ROSIE. Mum.

SUSAN. You're supposed to be helping me look for this bloody tape.

EVA *and* ARNOLD *enter.* ARNOLD *is covered in earth.*

EVA. Susan and Rosie are here.

ARNOLD. Yes I can see that.

EVA. Won't you say hello?

He won't.

PAUL. Hello, Arnold.

Neither will ROSIE.

SUSAN. Are you well?

ARNOLD. I'm fine.

SUSAN. Mum says you're ill.

ARNOLD. Does she.

EVA. It's his heart.

SUSAN. She said you had a fight with the neighbours.

EVA. Did I?

ARNOLD. I wouldn't have called it a fight.

SUSAN. Is it really a good idea for you to be gardening?

ARNOLD. We had a disagreement over the boundaries.

SUSAN. I mean it can be very strenuous, gardening.

ARNOLD. I'm not a cripple.

SUSAN. No. But the stairs. It's the stairs, isn't it? That are the problem.

EVA. There's a lift you see.

SUSAN. Still. It's a big upheaval.

ARNOLD. We'll manage.

SUSAN. Have you exchanged?

EVA. Have we what?

SUSAN. Has it all gone through?

ARNOLD. Yes.

SUSAN. Right. Good. Well.

EVA. Will you have some *Lebkuchen*?

ARNOLD. In a minute.

EVA. Rosie?

ROSIE. You already asked me.

EVA. Marzipan?

SUSAN. She's hungover.

ROSIE. I'm not.

EVA. You poor thing.

Aren't you pretty.

Isn't she pretty, Arnold.

No answer.

Isn't she pretty with her dark hair.

SUSAN. Must get it from her grandfather.

EVA. What?

SUSAN. The dark hair.

EVA. Yes, Harry was awfully dark. It was dreadful, everybody used to think he was an African.

SUSAN. Everybody did not.

EVA. Oh they did.

SUSAN. He wasn't that dark.

ARNOLD. He was a Sephardi which is just as bad.

SUSAN. There was nothing bad about my father.

ROSIE. Is Arnold being racist?

PAUL. Stop it, Rosie.

EVA. He was a marvellous actor.

ROSIE. Stop telling me to stop it.

EVA. But it was dreadful because he used to make everybody corpse. What was that play we did? Arnold?

ARNOLD. How should I know?

EVA. The Jew of somewhere or other. Anyway, they had to bring the curtain down one night we were laughing so much.

SUSAN. It was infectious, his laugh.

EVA. Somebody's writing a book about him.

SUSAN. About Dad?

EVA. Yes.

ARNOLD. No.

EVA. No?

ARNOLD. No, you're getting confused.

EVA. Am I?

ARNOLD. You mean *your* father.

EVA. My father, yes. Writing a book about him.

ARNOLD. Well. He features in it.

EVA. We had to give them the letters.

SUSAN. You gave away his letters?

ARNOLD. Copies.

SUSAN. Oh.

EVA. This fellow's been giving talks about it.

SUSAN. Which fellow?

EVA. You know. The one from the Jewish Museum.

ARNOLD. He'll talk about it to anyone. Anyone who'll listen.

SUSAN. Well it's

It's important. To remember.

ARNOLD. He even gave a talk to the football team.

EVA. Well they say they'll all be dead in ten years.

ARNOLD. Survivors she means. Not the England squad.

PAUL. Thank God for that.

SUSAN. Not funny, Paul.

PAUL. Oh come on.

EVA. Everybody wants to talk about it because they'll all be dead in ten years.

Silence.

SUSAN. I'd like copies of his letters.

EVA. Do we have the letters, Arnold?

ARNOLD. Somewhere, yes.

SUSAN. I'd like to get them translated.

EVA. Haven't you seen them?

SUSAN. Yes I've seen them but I can't read them.

EVA. Can't you?

SUSAN. You know I can't.

EVA. I could've taught you.

SUSAN. Yes, you could have.

EVA. Never mind.

SUSAN. Have you found it yet, Rosie?

ROSIE. I don't know where to start.

ARNOLD. Found what.

EVA. Susan wants a tape.

SUSAN. A tape I made with Mum.

EVA. Do we have it, Arnold?

ARNOLD. I don't know.

EVA. Arnold says we don't have it.

SUSAN. What?

EVA. Arnold says

SUSAN. No Mum, Arnold says he doesn't know, because Arnold wasn't here when we made the recording.

EVA. I can't remember.

ARNOLD. So there's a question of its existence, is there?

SUSAN. No, no question about that.

A cassette, you know, an old audio tape.

ARNOLD. Yes I know what they look like.

EVA. We've got hundreds of tapes.

ROSIE. What does the label say?

SUSAN. I don't know. Mum, Eva, something like that.

ARNOLD. We don't have anything that says Something Like That.

SUSAN. Put aside any blank ones too. In case the label's come off. I mean it was almost ten years ago so it's possible, you know, that the label's come off or it's got mixed up or…

ARNOLD. I really think you're wasting your time.

ROSIE *continues to look.*

SUSAN. It's important. To me. Something to have. To keep.

It's really all I want and if you must move well this seems like the perfect time. Not to move I mean to find it. I mean if it's not here then it's not going to be anywhere.

But it did happen. It happened, I'm not making it up. I remember very clearly, I remember the stories and the singing. *Omi* and *Opa* and Mrs Lyons and

I remember you talked and talked and it was the only time you'd ever talked like that.

And now you say you don't remember and well even if you don't. I want to. Remember.

It's important to me.

I mean if you're throwing it all out anyway…

Silence.

EVA. Oh dear.

SUSAN. What.

EVA. I forgot to make the tea.

SUSAN. It's all right.

EVA. You came for tea, didn't you?

PAUL. Yes.

SUSAN. But it's all right.

ARNOLD *is about to exit*.

EVA. Arnold?

ARNOLD. What is it.

EVA. I forgot to make the tea.

ROSIE *picks up a tape*.

ROSIE. Is it this one?

SUSAN. What does it say?

ROSIE. Mum 2002.

SUSAN. Yes, it must be.

ARNOLD. Are you sure?

SUSAN. Of course I'm sure, look it's my writing.

PAUL. Good. That's that then.

EVA. Arnold?

ARNOLD. I think we should check it.

EVA. He wants to check it.

SUSAN. Why?

ARNOLD. Because I wasn't aware that you'd made such a tape.

SUSAN. Well, we did.

ARNOLD. Well, I'd like to be sure.

EVA. We've got a what's-it somewhere.

ROSIE. A cassette player.

EVA. That's right.

PAUL. Jesus.

SUSAN. Is this really necessary? If you're throwing it all out anyway?

EVA. Is it necessary, Arnold?

ARNOLD starts looking in one of the boxes.

SUSAN. I mean I'll just take it home and

I can make copies for you. I can send it off and you know, have it

What's it called, Rosie?

ROSIE. Digitised.

SUSAN. Right, and then I can burn it, to CDs.

ARNOLD finds an old cassette player.

ARNOLD. Well go on.

SUSAN hesitates, then puts the tape in the machine and presses 'Play'.

They wait.

SUSAN. I don't like the noise it's making.

EVA. It's ever so old.

ARNOLD. I'll do it.

ARNOLD takes over.

SUSAN. Do what?

ARNOLD. You might have inserted it incorrectly.

SUSAN. I did not insert it incorrectly.

ARNOLD. There's a knack.

SUSAN. It's at the end of a side.

ARNOLD. Then it needs turning around.

SUSAN. Just press 'Rewind'.

ARNOLD. No it's the button, it won't

SUSAN tries to help.

I'll do it, I'm doing it.

SUSAN. I really don't like the noise it's making.

Paul?

ARNOLD *smacks the machine*.

(*To* ARNOLD.) What are you doing?

ARNOLD. I'm trying to open it.

SUSAN. By hitting it?

ARNOLD. It won't open.

SUSAN. What d'you mean won't open.

ARNOLD. It's stuck.

SUSAN. Paul.

PAUL. What.

ROSIE. Let me try.

ARNOLD. I'm doing it.

SUSAN. Let her, Arnold, she's got smaller fingers than you.

ARNOLD. I told you, there's a knack.

EVA. It's ever so old.

ARNOLD. Although I have a feeling it might be broken.

SUSAN. The tape?

ARNOLD. The machine.

EVA. Oh dear.

SUSAN. Is that why it's up here? Because you're throwing it out?

ROSIE. Well nobody listens to tapes any more.

ARNOLD. I'll get a screwdriver.

SUSAN. This is ridiculous.

ARNOLD. Don't touch anything, I'm getting a screwdriver.

ARNOLD *exits*.

SUSAN. Screwdriver, I mean really.

EVA. He wants to check it.

SUSAN. Yes. I know.

EVA. He's terribly ill.

SUSAN. Then he shouldn't be running around looking for bloody screwdrivers, should he.

EVA. What a mess.

SUSAN. Quite apart from the fact that it has nothing to do with him.

EVA. All these boxes.

SUSAN. It's *your* life on that tape.

EVA. All this stuff.

SUSAN. He just can't bear the thought of me having anything at all.

EVA. Will you have some marzipan?

SUSAN. Not a lot to ask for, is it? A tape? One tape?

EVA. A piece of chocolate?

SUSAN. No Mum, I don't want any fucking chocolate.

PAUL. Calm down, Susan.

SUSAN. And why are you just sitting there?

PAUL. What do you want me to do?

SUSAN. Rosie's hungover and you're just sitting there.

ROSIE. *I* found the tape.

SUSAN. Yes and now it's bloody stuck.

EVA. Oh dear.

SUSAN. Quite.

Silence.

ARNOLD *enters with a screwdriver.*

EVA. Arnold? Marzipan?

ARNOLD. In a minute.

He starts fiddling with the cassette player.

SUSAN. Be careful.

ARNOLD. I know what I'm doing.

SUSAN. They're fragile things, tapes.

ARNOLD. I'm quite capable.

They watch ARNOLD *prise open its cover.*

SUSAN. I mean you've got to be careful because the sound quality deteriorates over time and

EVA *applauds as* ARNOLD *removes the tape from the machine.*

EVA. *Bravo*. Aren't you clever.

SUSAN. All right, I'll check it at home.

It's my tape, Arnold.

ARNOLD. Actually we're not sure whose tape it is.

SUSAN. But it's almost certainly *my tape*.

ARNOLD. But we don't know that.

SUSAN. We do know that because it's got my handwriting on the cover.

PAUL. For God's sake, let him check the damn thing.

SUSAN. …

ARNOLD. There's a cassette player in the car.

SUSAN. It works, does it?

ARNOLD. I believe so.

SUSAN. Fine. I'll come with you.

ARNOLD. That won't be necessary.

ARNOLD dusts himself off and exits with the tape.

SUSAN. This is ridiculous.

EVA. He wants to go on his own.

SUSAN. I heard him, Mum.

EVA. He wants to check it.

SUSAN. *I know*.

EVA. I don't want any trouble.

Silence.

ROSIE. So what. Now we just… wait?

Blackout.

Three

2014

The Kreuzberg apartment. Tidier this time, the suitcase out of sight.

It's late morning. SUSAN *and* PAUL *have just arrived.* ROSIE *hovers.*

SUSAN. I thought I was going to die. Didn't I, Paul? I actually thought we were all going to die.

PAUL. Well…

SUSAN. It got *stuck* can you believe.

PAUL. The lift.

SUSAN. There was this jolt, this tremendous jolt and then it just… stopped.

ROSIE. But you didn't die.

PAUL. No.

SUSAN. Twenty or more of us squeezed together like sardines and nobody knew what the hell was going on and you know what I'm like in confined spaces.

ROSIE. …

SUSAN. Well I've developed a terrible fear of confined spaces and we were just hanging there suspended in mid-air for what seemed like hours.

PAUL. It was a long five minutes.

SUSAN. Hours and hours until eventually there was a German voice on the intercom which of course nobody understood and some poor chap had to translate the whole bloody thing. And what with the jolt and the intercom and the lack of oxygen, well I worked myself up into such a state that by the time we reached the top I'd completely lost my appetite. Couldn't eat a thing.

ROSIE. Oh. Well Sebastian's getting cake so

SUSAN. Peppermint tea and a Valium was all I could manage.

PAUL. Incredible view though.

SUSAN. Completely spoilt what's been a lovely little trip.

PAUL. Not *completely*.

SUSAN. No I mean apart from that it's been a lovely little trip.

ROSIE. Good.

SUSAN. We did everything on the list, didn't we.

PAUL. Yup. Packed a lot in.

SUSAN. Television Tower, Checkpoint Charlie, Jewish Museum…

Feel like I need a holiday.

Are you all right, Rosie? You're awfully quiet. Are you hungover?

ROSIE. No, Mum.

SUSAN. Don't want you being sick on the plane.

ROSIE. I'm not hungover, I'm just

SUSAN. …

THREE   35

ROSIE. Look. I don't know how to say this but

SEBASTIAN *enters with a Lidl bag.*

SEBASTIAN. Hi.

SUSAN. Hello again, Sebastian.

SEBASTIAN. Welcome.

PAUL. Nice place you've got.

SEBASTIAN. Thanks.

PAUL. Reminds me of a squat I used to live in back in the eighties.

SUSAN. Paul.

PAUL. No I mean you know, the warehouse vibe.

SEBASTIAN. Right, sure.

SEBASTIAN *takes a packet of* Lebkuchen *from the Lidl bag.*

Lebkuchen?

SUSAN. Oh.

SEBASTIAN. German biscuits.

ROSIE. She knows what they are.

SEBASTIAN. Of course.

SUSAN. Yes, my mother used to buy them.

He rips open the packet and tips them into a bowl.

SEBASTIAN. *Hast du schon etwas gesagt?* [Have you said anything yet?]

ROSIE. No.

SUSAN. Aren't you wonderful, going out especially. Here, let me give you some money for it, how much did it cost.

SEBASTIAN. No, please.

SUSAN. No really, I know what it must be like for you struggling artists.

ROSIE. Do you?

SUSAN. Well no, I can only imagine. Terrible.

SEBASTIAN. Please. I insist.

ROSIE. Actually Sebastian's getting paid for his art. He's getting money for ideas that are in his head.

SUSAN. Oh yes, Rosie says you've got a commission.

SEBASTIAN. For an installation, yeah.

SUSAN. In an old bunker she said.

SEBASTIAN. Uh-huh.

ROSIE. Site-specific.

SUSAN. Such a shame we're missing it.

PAUL. What's it about?

SEBASTIAN. Uh…

ROSIE. Sebastian hates that question.

PAUL. If you had to describe it in one sentence.

SEBASTIAN. No, okay, I'd say it's

it's a digital simulation of

of life and death.

PAUL. Nice and cheery then.

SUSAN. Paul.

PAUL. I was joking, I was making a joke.

SEBASTIAN. No, sure, it's depressing. But also uplifting. Maybe.

It's looking at like, patterns of evolution, how generations expand or die out. Like, how individuals make up a collective, and then how the actions of the collective feed back to the individuals.

So I'm experimenting with, um, looping and digital motion capture to create a kind of zooming-out effect, you know?

Like does the individual get lost when it becomes part of a swarm? When hours become seconds or years become minutes or

SUSAN. Like me in the lift.

SEBASTIAN. I'm sorry?

ROSIE. No, the other way round.

PAUL. Sounds like a 'have to be there' sort of thing.

SEBASTIAN. It's basically asking whether we can look at our history with any objectivity.

SUSAN. And? Can we?

SEBASTIAN. I don't know, it's posing a question.

SUSAN. No I just mean

well the answer seems fairly straightforward to me.

SEBASTIAN. Does it?

SUSAN. Well yes. If it's history then it's there. It's happened. Whatever we feel about it.

SEBASTIAN. But then history itself is subjective, no?

SUSAN. No.

I mean I'm sure it's all very interesting and atmospheric, but personally I don't need an exhibition

ROSIE. Installation.

SUSAN. to ask me whether or not I can look at my own history objectively.

SEBASTIAN. For sure.

But I think sometimes it's impossible to judge when you're right in the middle of it. Of time. I mean we don't even know where we are. We might be at the end. Or the beginning.

Anyway. I'm not explaining it well.

It's a bit of a fuck-head at the moment.

ROSIE. Head-fuck.

SEBASTIAN. Yeah, that.

Silence.

SUSAN. Has Rosie shown you the letter?

ROSIE. Yes.

SEBASTIAN. What?

SUSAN. At the Jewish Museum.

ROSIE. Yeah you've seen it, on the lower level.

SEBASTIAN. Right, by the outside bit.

ROSIE. Garden of Exile.

SEBASTIAN. Right.

SUSAN. It's a letter from my mother's father. To his wife, my mother's mother. They never saw each other again.

That's history, that is. That's history you can hold in your hand.

Silence.

They had a translation up on the wall.

(*To* ROSIE.) I don't expect you need a translation now, do you.

ROSIE. No. But still. His handwriting.

SUSAN. Strange. Seeing it in a glass case.

ROSIE. Zooming in.

SUSAN. What?

Do you know much about Rosie's history?

ROSIE. I showed him the letter.

SEBASTIAN. She… yes, she showed me the letter.

SUSAN. There was a tape. We made it. My mother and I. I interviewed her.

Silence.

(*To* ROSIE.) You should visit.

ROSIE. I will.

SUSAN. She's always asking for you.

ROSIE. I know.

SUSAN. Constantly asking for her granddaughter.

ROSIE. Does she like the home?

SUSAN. It has a nice garden.

ROSIE. Good.

Good.

SUSAN. But you know.

ROSIE. Yeah.

SUSAN. You really should visit.

ROSIE. I plan to.

Silence.

PAUL *picks up a newspaper.* SUSAN *takes a biscuit.*

SEBASTIAN. *Und? Wirst du was sagen?* [Well? Are you going to say something?]

ROSIE. In a minute.

SUSAN. Rosie had a bad experience with *Lebkuchen*.

ROSIE. I think I'm allergic.

SUSAN. She ate too many.

ROSIE. Allergic I said.

SUSAN. Drank too much and ate too many biscuits.

ROSIE. Mum.

SUSAN. I hope you've been keeping an eye on her, Sebastian.

ROSIE. An eye on me?

SUSAN. Well I worry.

ROSIE. About what?

SUSAN. You know.

ROSIE. No I don't.

SUSAN. And it's worse when you're in another country.

ROSIE. What is?

SUSAN. Isn't it, Paul.

PAUL. Hmm?

SUSAN. My anxiety.

PAUL. What? Yes, but she's coming home.

SUSAN. Thank God.

PAUL. So no more panic attacks.

ROSIE. Panic attacks?

SUSAN. I know it's not rational.

ROSIE. Well no but since when have you

SUSAN. But you never call.

ROSIE. It's expensive.

SUSAN. Never pick up.

ROSIE. Nobody uses house phones any more.

SUSAN. I do. I'm not a Nobody.

ROSIE. If you'd just download Skype then

SUSAN. Well I don't need to now, do I.

Silence.

ROSIE *starts eating from the bowl of* Lebkuchen.

SEBASTIAN. *Glaubst du nicht, dass du was dazu sagen solltest?* [Don't you think you should say something?]

ROSIE. *Ich warte auf den richtigen Zeitpunkt.* [I'm waiting for the right moment.]

SEBASTIAN. *Aber je länger du wartest…* [But the longer you leave it…]

SUSAN. What's he talking about?

ROSIE. *Ich werde verdammt noch mal nichts sagen, nachdem sie mir gerade von ihren Panikattacken und ihrem schlechten Zustand erzählt hat.* [I'm not going to say something when she's just told me what a state she's been in, when she's just told me she's having panic attacks for fuck's sake.]

SUSAN. Rosie?

SEBASTIAN. *Und ich dachte, du wärst allergisch gegen Lebkuchen.* [And I thought you said you were allergic to *Lebkuchen*.]

ROSIE. He says he thought I was allergic to *Lebkuchen*.

SUSAN. Oh don't be silly, nobody's allergic to *Lebkuchen*.

SEBASTIAN. *Wenn du nichts sagst werde ich etwas sagen.* [If you don't say something then I will.]

ROSIE. *Ich hab's dir doch gesagt, ich warte auf den richtigen Zeitpunkt.* [I told you, I'm waiting for the right moment.]

SUSAN. Paul, they keep speaking in German.

ROSIE. *Und hör auf Deutsch zu reden, das ist echt unhöflich.* [And stop speaking in German, it's really rude.]

PAUL. The wonderful thing about Sudoku is that you can make sense of it whichever country you're in.

SEBASTIAN. *Wie du willst. Ich warte bis du den 'richtigen Zeitpunkt' gefunden hast. Scheiße.* [Fine. I'll leave you to find the 'right moment'. Fuck.]

SEBASTIAN *exits.*

ROSIE *picks up the bowl and continues to eat.*

SUSAN. It's okay, darling. Slow down. Give me the *Lebkuchen*. That's right, give it to me.

She lets SUSAN *take the bowl.*

Now. What's the matter. He's in a bad mood, isn't he.

ROSIE. The thing is…

SUSAN. He's upset because you're leaving.

PAUL. We should think about making a move soon.

SUSAN. Okay Paul, I'm thinking about it.

ROSIE. The thing

   I just

   The thing is…

SUSAN. Where are your cases, Rosie?

   No answer.

   Rosie? Where are your things?

   No answer.

   Paul, will you help Rosie with her things?

   Paul?

ROSIE. I'm not leaving.

   I'm staying. For my final year. And then. We'll see.

SUSAN. PAUL?

   PAUL *slams down the newspaper.*

PAUL. WHAT? WHAT DO YOU WANT ME TO DO?

   Silence.

   SUSAN *gets up and looks out the window.*

   (*To* ROSIE.) You've looked into it, have you?

ROSIE. What?

PAUL. Staying? For your final year?

ROSIE. Sort of.

PAUL. Well have you or haven't you?

ROSIE. What's it got to do with you?

PAUL. A lot actually.

ROSIE. My father's the one paying the fees.

PAUL. And your mother is losing her goddamn mind.

Silence.

SUSAN. She wants to stay.

PAUL. Well. She's an adult. It's her decision.

SUSAN. She doesn't love me.

ROSIE. Mum.

Mum I didn't know you were

PAUL. You really pick your moments, don't you. I mean you could've told us I dunno, when we arrived and not two hours before we're due to catch a bloody plane. Who knows, maybe then your mother would've scheduled in more time to see you instead of cramming in bus tours and museums and breakfasts at the top of the bloody Reichstag.

ROSIE. I'm sorry.

PAUL. You're a selfish cow sometimes, Rosie.

SUSAN. Paul. Don't.

PAUL. Complete disregard for anyone but yourself.

ROSIE. I'm not a child, Paul, you can't tell me off for wanting to live in another country, all right?

PAUL. It's this lack of self-awareness that really

I've said, I've said before, this this this inability to

ROSIE. It's not my fault that Mum worries.

PAUL. There you go again.

ROSIE. I didn't know how bad

PAUL. And shoving it in her face, the German

SUSAN. Paul, it's okay.

PAUL. when you know she can't speak it no it's not okay. You know what she's going through with her own mother.

SUSAN. Paul.

PAUL. I mean what are you trying to do to her?

SUSAN. Don't.

PAUL. What are you trying to do to *us*?

Silence.

SUSAN. Look at the time.

ROSIE. I didn't mean to tell you like this.

SUSAN. We'd better get in the taxi, hadn't we.

ROSIE. Please, can we just

SUSAN. No Rosie, I can't. Not right now.

PAUL. I'll be downstairs.

SEBASTIAN enters as PAUL is about to exit.

Good luck. With the installation and

Yup.

PAUL exits.

SEBASTIAN hovers for a moment, then exits.

ROSIE. I'm sorry.

SUSAN is about to exit, then stops.

SUSAN. What is it you're running from?

ROSIE. I'm not running from anything.

SUSAN. Is it me?

ROSIE. I'm not

SUSAN. Yes you are, you do this, this is what you do, you've done this since you were a little girl. Paul says it's because

ROSIE. Oh for fuck's sake.

Sorry.

I don't know.

There's something that pulls me here. I can't explain it but it feels

It's not home exactly, not like London, but then London doesn't always feel like a home either. And at the end of the day we're talking about bricks and mortar and which side of the road you drive on but still. Something pulls me here.

Sebastian, yes, but not just Sebastian.

I'm starting to dream in German. I used to hear people say that, that they'd start dreaming in a language, and how when that happens it means it's finally become a part of you and

I suppose that's happening to me.

Well I'm half-German, aren't I? Technically?

SUSAN. It's complicated.

ROSIE. Yeah. Well.

Maybe I have to go back to move forward. And maybe I should just go with my gut, you know? My heart. Instead of always doing what I planned. What anyone planned.

I know it's bad I haven't seen Grandma. I think about her a lot. And you, obviously, obviously I think about you all a lot.

It's not for ever. It's not. It's just for another year or so or *I don't know* but I don't want to live in a shoebox and really, aside from you and Grandma, really, what's keeping me in London? I've got friends here too now. And Skype. So.

So yeah. I think this is. My home. For a while at least.

Silence.

SEBASTIAN *enters.*

SEBASTIAN. Susan. I feel I should

SUSAN (*to* ROSIE). Love you, darling.

Always loved you.

She kisses ROSIE *on the cheek.*

You can't say it. Can you. To me.

Does she say it to you, Sebastian?

No answer.

Do visit your grandmother. Or call her at least.

Puts down the bowl of Lebkuchen.

And do pick up from time to time.

...and exits.

SEBASTIAN *goes to* ROSIE. *He holds her tight.*

Fade to blackout.

The answerphone beep.

EVA (*voice-over*). Rosie? Are you there?

Rosie they've come with the shears. They're cutting it all down. They said it'll grow back but I'm not sure it will.

Can you check?

Rosie?

I'm worried about the men with the shears. First it was the flowers and now it's the hedge. First it was one man and now there are two of them. That's how these things happen.

They think I won't notice but I'm not stupid.

I don't trust them, Rosie.

Rosie?

Did I send you the cheque? Did you buy yourself something? I want to know if you're coming for Christmas. I need to know how much marzipan to make.

We have to stop them, Rosie. Before it's too late.

Click as the phone hangs up.

Four

2011

The attic in North London. Everything is as was, other than bowls of Lebkuchen, *marzipan and chocolate.*

Two hours have passed. ROSIE *is drinking red wine and looking through a pile of letters with* EVA.

ROSIE. Why don't you have an accent?

EVA. Well one couldn't. It wasn't fashionable.

ROSIE. D'you reckon they run in families?

EVA. Accents?

ROSIE. Languages.

EVA. I don't know.

ROSIE. Only one I was any good at in school.

EVA. Can you read it?

    ROSIE *looks at the letter.*

ROSIE. Yeah, no, not that good. Only word I understand in that sentence is *'ich'*.

EVA. Terrible, isn't it. He wrote like a doctor.

    (Reading.) Ich darf Ihnen nochmals schreiben.

ROSIE. …

EVA. It means 'I am permitted to write to you again'. Which means that at some point or other he wasn't. They screened them you see. One had to read between the lines.

    Quite remarkable that he managed to write at all.

ROSIE. What else does it say?

    EVA *looks closer.*

EVA. Says he misses chocolate.

ROSIE. Really? Chocolate?

EVA. *Schokolade mit Haselnüssen.*

ROSIE. Right, yeah, hazelnuts.

EVA. Will you have a piece?

ROSIE. What? No I…

Okay. I'll have a piece. One piece. Thanks.

ROSIE *breaks off a piece of chocolate and eats it slowly.*

EVA. Says he's having trouble with his glasses. They keep breaking or something.

Gebrochen. Means 'broken'.

SUSAN *enters.*

SUSAN. I can't find him.

EVA. Who?

SUSAN. Arnold. He must've gone for a drive.

EVA. He's not supposed to drive.

SUSAN. Well his car isn't there.

EVA. It's his heart.

SUSAN. Has he got a phone on him?

EVA. I shouldn't think so.

SUSAN. He's been two hours.

ROSIE. He's screening it.

SUSAN. Are you drinking?

ROSIE. So?

SUSAN. So it's a bit early for wine.

EVA. Let her drink the wine.

ROSIE *starts helping herself to the* Lebkuchen *and marzipan.*

SUSAN. Well. This is perfect. Arnold's buggered off, Rosie's started drinking and Paul's downstairs playing bloody Sudoku.

ROSIE. 'Rosie's started drinking.'

SUSAN. And save some room for supper.

ROSIE. I'm hungry.

EVA. She's hungry.

ROSIE. Starving.

EVA. She's ever so slim.

SUSAN. Yes, well, doesn't mean she should fill up on biscuits.

EVA. She needs to eat more.

SUSAN. She'll make herself sick.

EVA (*to* ROSIE). Have some more *Lebkuchen*.

SUSAN. She does that sometimes.

ROSIE. Mum.

SUSAN. Makes herself sick.

ROSIE. I am here you know.

EVA. Let her eat the *Lebkuchen*.

ROSIE *pushes the bowl away and gets up*.

SUSAN. Where are you going?

ROSIE. For a cigarette.

She exits.

SUSAN. D'you see what I have to put up with?

EVA. Poor thing.

SUSAN. *I'm* the poor thing, it's *me* who's the poor thing.

EVA. Oh stop it.

SUSAN. What a nightmare.

Bloody farce.

EVA. Well you shouldn't have sent him off in the car.

SUSAN. I didn't send him off anywhere.

EVA. He's not supposed to drive.

SUSAN. I wasn't given much of a choice.

EVA. It's his heart.

SUSAN. You're repeating yourself.

EVA. The doctor said

SUSAN. You keep

What? What did the doctor say?

EVA. That he's not supposed to drive.

SUSAN. But what about *you*?

EVA. I never liked driving anyway.

SUSAN. Have you been for tests, Mum?

EVA. I like being driven.

SUSAN. Mum.

EVA. There's nothing wrong with me.

SUSAN. You couldn't remember the tomatoes.

EVA. It's Arnold.

SUSAN. Or the tape.

EVA. It's his heart.

SUSAN. Yes, his heart his heart, I'm talking about *you*.

You really can't remember making it?

EVA. The bolognese?

SUSAN. The recording. The interview.

EVA. I can't remember.

SUSAN. I'm going to go mad in a minute.

PAUL *enters*.

I am actually going to go mad.

PAUL. Are we done?

SUSAN. No we are not done. Arnold's checking the bloody thing, God knows where he is.

EVA. There's a what's-it in the car.

SUSAN. I'm starting to worry he'll hear something he doesn't like and drive himself into a ditch.

PAUL. Unlikely.

SUSAN. And Mum can't remember.

EVA. Well she shouldn't have sent him off in the car.

SUSAN. Or won't remember or

EVA. There's nothing wrong with me.

SUSAN. or I don't know but I'm about to get into a terrible state.

PAUL. Listen.

SUSAN. And you're not exactly helping.

PAUL. Calm down.

SUSAN. Disappearing for two hours to play Sudoku, I mean really.

ROSIE *enters*.

And Rosie with her drinking and her cigarettes and her

ROSIE. Arnold's back.

SUSAN. What?

ROSIE. I saw his car pull in.

PAUL. Hasn't driven himself into a ditch then.

ROSIE *goes back to the marzipan*.

SUSAN. Is this kind of thing normal? Does this kind of thing happen in *normal* families? People driving off with tapes

I mean is there this level of

Rosie will you STOP. EATING.

ROSIE *stops mid-mouthful*.

EVA. Shall I make some

SUSAN. No stop it okay no. No tea. Thank you.

Silence.

ARNOLD *enters.*

EVA. Susan and Rosie are here.

PAUL. I'll be downstairs.

PAUL *exits.*

SUSAN. Where did you go?

No answer.

Mum says you're not supposed to drive.

ARNOLD. Does she.

SUSAN. Yes.

ARNOLD. I see.

SUSAN. Well?

ARNOLD. Well what.

SUSAN. Is it? The tape?

ARNOLD. It is a tape, yes.

SUSAN. Here we go.

ARNOLD. But it's not the tape you're looking for.

SUSAN. How much of it did you listen to?

ARNOLD. You see, I was right to check it because it isn't the tape you're looking for.

SUSAN. But it must be.

ARNOLD. Are you calling me a liar?

SUSAN. No Arnold, not a liar, no, no I'm trying to find out whether you listened to all of it or whether

ARNOLD. I heard enough.

SUSAN. Because I mean some of it could've been taped over or or

ARNOLD. I said I heard enough.

SUSAN. So what is it then.

ARNOLD. If you must know it's a recording of *The Archers*.

SUSAN. ...

He's joking. No this is a joke. You're joking, aren't you, tell me you're joking.

ARNOLD. Do I look like I'm joking?

SUSAN. *The Archers*?

ARNOLD. That is what I said.

SUSAN. I mean fuck, I mean so you

so someone

Someone taped over it. Or part of it. But some of it could still be on there.

Some of it could still be on there, no?

No answer.

No. Right. So that's...

That's that then.

Silence.

EVA (*to* ARNOLD). Will you have some marzipan?

ARNOLD. Yes all right.

ROSIE. I finished it.

EVA. Oh dear.

ROSIE. Sorry.

EVA. We'd better get some more.

ROSIE. Is there more wine?

EVA. In the kitchen, will you help me?

SUSAN. She really doesn't need any more wine.

ROSIE. Nobody *needs* wine.

EVA. Come on.

EVA and ROSIE exit.

Silence.

SUSAN. Are you going to tell me what's wrong with my mother?

ARNOLD. There's nothing wrong with her.

SUSAN. It's getting worse.

ARNOLD. I don't know what you're talking about.

SUSAN. Forgetting things. Repeating herself.

ARNOLD. It's what happens.

SUSAN. I want to take her for tests.

ARNOLD. She's been for tests.

SUSAN. What?

You didn't tell me.

ARNOLD. I'm telling you now.

SUSAN. So what did they say?

ARNOLD. The results were inconclusive. They don't know.

SUSAN. But I mean

it could be

Something.

Could it?

ARNOLD. It's too early to say.

SUSAN. I want to

It's important that I

I want to know these things.

ARNOLD. Really? You seem more interested in a cassette tape.

SUSAN. Arnold. Please.

Silence.

ARNOLD. She's on a trial.

SUSAN. What sort of trial?

ARNOLD. You know. Drugs.

SUSAN. ...

ARNOLD. Reminyl.

SUSAN. And? Is it working?

ARNOLD. As I told you, it's too early to say.

In any case it only treats the symptoms.

SUSAN. Why? *Why* didn't you tell me?

ARNOLD. What difference would it make?

SUSAN. I have a right to know. A right to know about my mother before she

ARNOLD. Before she what. Forgets she has a daughter?

SUSAN. Well what am I supposed to think when you

when you withhold information from me.

I supposed it suits you, doesn't it. This. Her forgetting things.

ARNOLD. I look after your mother.

SUSAN. Look after? You're making it worse. Much much worse. Moving house is disorientating for someone of her age, of your age, I mean for someone in her condition.

London is her home.

ARNOLD. London is where we ended up.

Silence.

SUSAN *inhales, as if about to speak.*

Why do you want this tape so much?

SUSAN. Because

ARNOLD. What is it you want to remember?

SUSAN. Because it's all I've got left of my

ARNOLD. No. You want it as proof. As ammunition.

SUSAN. What's that supposed to mean?

No answer.

Arnold?

Have you listened to it?

Have you?

EVA *and* ROSIE *enter.* ROSIE *is wearing a fur jacket.*

EVA. Doesn't she look marvellous.

ROSIE. It's vintage. From the sixties.

SUSAN. Yes. Very nice.

ROSIE. Grandma says I can keep it.

SUSAN. That's very kind.

EVA. Isn't she pretty, Arnold.

No answer.

ROSIE *poses with her glass of wine.*

ROSIE. Am I, Arnold? Pretty?

SUSAN. Rosie.

EVA. With her lovely dark hair.

PAUL *enters.*

PAUL. Jesus, what are you wearing?

ROSIE. It's vintage.

PAUL. Are we done? We should think about making a move.

EVA. But you haven't had any tea.

PAUL. I don't think you made any, Eva.

EVA. Didn't I?

ROSIE. We're onto wine now.

FOUR 57

PAUL. But we really should think about

SUSAN. Yes all right, Paul.

EVA. Did you want anything?

PAUL. D'you mean tea or stuff or

EVA. The Wagner?

PAUL. No thank you.

SUSAN. Why would we want Wagner? Why do you even have Wagner?

ROSIE. What's wrong with Wagner?

SUSAN. They won't play Wagner in Israel you know.

PAUL *rolls his eyes*.

EVA. So you don't want the Wagner.

SUSAN. No.

EVA. They don't want anything.

SUSAN. Actually. Actually, you know what I want? What I really want is an episode or two of *The Archers*.

PAUL. What?

SUSAN. Yup, any episode, long as it's old.

PAUL. Come on, Susan, we really don't need any more stuff.

SUSAN. It's not too much to ask. Take what you like, that's what you said. Well I'd like *The Archers*.

EVA. Do we have it, Arnold?

ROSIE. Mum. *The Archers* is shit.

EVA. Arnold?

SUSAN. I'm not going to make a scene. I just want that tape.

Arnold. Give me the tape.

He doesn't.

Give me the fucking tape.

He doesn't.

SUSAN *pounces. There is a struggle.*

PAUL. Susan

SUSAN. You

You

Give me the

Give me the fucking

LET GO.

PAUL. Susan just calm down just stop that just

SUSAN. It's *her* life on there. *Her* life. It has *nothing* to do with you.

Nothing.

Before she can take it, ARNOLD *rips the reels of tape from inside its casing and throws it to the floor.*

ARNOLD. THERE.

Nobody moves.

Nothing.

SUSAN *kneels on the floor and gathers the reels of tape in her hands.* ROSIE *downs her glass of wine.* PAUL *inhales, as if about to speak.*

Why does everybody want to

Suddenly ARNOLD *clutches his chest.*

talk about it all the

Stumbles to find a seat.

EVA. Arnold? Are you all right?

Arnold?

ARNOLD. I'm fine.

PAUL. You don't look fine.

EVA. D'you want to go to the hospital?

ARNOLD. No.

PAUL. No come on, I'll drive you there now.

EVA. D'you want to go, Arnold?

PAUL. Seriously, what if you're

ARNOLD. I said no.

EVA. It could be the what's-it.

PAUL. The what?

EVA. The acid what's-it.

PAUL. Acid reflux?

EVA. The indigestion.

PAUL. Are you sure?

EVA. Are you sure, Arnold?

ARNOLD. I can hear perfectly well, thank you.

EVA. He says he can hear.

PAUL. Listen. Arnold. Let me drive you to the hospital.

ARNOLD. That won't be necessary.

PAUL. Just for peace of mind.

ARNOLD. I'm quite all right.

PAUL. Please. I'd never forgive myself if

ARNOLD. I am *quite all right*.

ARNOLD composes himself and stands.

Excuse me.

PAUL steps out the way. ARNOLD *exits.*

PAUL. D'you think I should? Drive him?

EVA. I don't know.

PAUL. I'm happy to.

SUSAN. For God's sake, Paul, leave it, he said he's fine.

PAUL. Didn't look fine to me.

SUSAN. What are you a doctor now? You heard, it's acid fucking reflux, he eats too much.

ROSIE *starts laughing*.

PAUL. Don't laugh, Rosie.

...but she can't stop.

EVA. What? What's so funny? What is it?

ROSIE *is having a full-on giggle fit.* EVA *starts laughing at* ROSIE *laughing*.

SUSAN *buries her head in the reels of tape and starts to sob.* PAUL *goes to her and she clings to him until the sobbing stops and the giggles subside and all three women have tears in their eyes of some sort.*

PAUL. Come on. Let's go.

SUSAN *gets to her feet.*

SUSAN. Have you written down the new address?

EVA. You'd better ask Arnold.

SUSAN. Right.

EVA. I don't want any trouble.

SUSAN. No.

EVA. It's easier. There's a lift.

SUSAN. You said.

EVA *shakes her head in bemusement.*

EVA. I can't understand it.

SUSAN. What.

EVA. I can't understand why they killed my father.

Silence.

He must have done something awfully stupid. I mean he would have got out.

Silence.

SUSAN. No. Of course. Of course you can't.

Silence.

EVA. You'd better go.

He'll sulk.

SUSAN. ...

PAUL. Are you ready, Rosie?

ROSIE. ...

EVA. Do you need some money?

ROSIE. What? No. I mean... yeah. Money's always... useful.

EVA. Where's my chequebook?

She starts looking for it.

ROSIE. But it's fine.

EVA. Is fifty pounds enough?

ROSIE. Like if you can't find it.

EVA. A hundred?

ROSIE. Yeah but

we can sort it out another time.

EVA. Can we?

ROSIE. Yeah.

EVA. Will you buy yourself something from me?

ROSIE. Okay.

EVA. And I'll write you a cheque?

ROSIE. Okay.

EVA. Suits you.

ROSIE. What? Oh. The jacket. Yeah. Yeah I like it.

EVA. Lovely teeth.

ROSIE *holds her stomach.*

What's the matter?

ROSIE. …

    I think I'm going to be sick.

    She retches, then exits quickly.

EVA. Oh dear. Poor thing.

    Silence.

    EVA *turns away and looks at the boxes.*

PAUL. Bye, Eva. Thanks for the

    Yup.

    (*To* SUSAN.) I'll be in the car.

    PAUL *exits.*

    SUSAN *looks at the broken tape. Looks at her mother. Is about to reach for her. Changes her mind and exits.*

    Silence.

    EVA *looks around the room. Takes a few paces. Touches her toes.*

    She half-sings, half-hums, quietly:

EVA.
    Nun ade du mein lieb Heimatland, lieb Heimatland, ade
    Es geht jetzt fort zum fremden Strand, lieb Heimatland, ade

    ARNOLD *enters.*

ARNOLD. Eva?

    She stops. Turns around.

    Silence.

    It's like they are having separate conversations.

    Eva, I heard it.

EVA. Are you feeling better?

ARNOLD. I…

EVA. Is it the acid what's-it?

ARNOLD. I don't suppose you remember but

> but is it true? What you said?
>
> Not a single...

EVA. What?

ARNOLD. hair...

EVA. Are you all right?

ARNOLD. Eva?

> *Silence.*

EVA. We've got to be careful, haven't we. With your heart.

ARNOLD. Because it isn't true for me.

> Because I've always...

EVA. What?

He looks at her, but can't say it.

Blackout.

Five

2002

Somewhere in the house in North London.

SUSAN *and* EVA *sit with a tape recorder between them.* SUSAN *is fiddling with its settings.*

SUSAN. No I'm just *checking* that it hasn't, you know, switched off or something.

EVA. Do you want me to keep talking?

SUSAN. Yes but hold on I just

EVA. What do you want me to talk about?

SUSAN. There.

She looks up.

Just carry on from where we left off.

Is it difficult?

EVA. What?

SUSAN. To talk about it?

EVA. It's difficult to remember it all in the right order.

Why are we doing this?

SUSAN. Because… I want something to keep.

EVA. Okay. Well I suppose you want to know about the arrest.

Have I told you about the arrest?

SUSAN. Well a bit, but you're the one who's supposed to be

EVA. Talking, yes, okay.

Well. I was nine and I was there that day.

SUSAN. Which day?

EVA. I'm talking, Susan.

SUSAN. Yes all right, sorry, yes, talk.

EVA. I was there that day and

Really it was very unfortunate, I think a neighbour or somebody must have

I don't know, but it was very early in the morning and

SUSAN *starts fiddling with the tape recorder again.*

What are you doing?

SUSAN. I'm just making sure that I didn't

EVA. Is it recording?

SUSAN. Yes I think so I just

EVA. I don't want to have to repeat myself.

SUSAN. No I think it's fine, yes, go on.

EVA. So they came very early in the morning and

SUSAN. Who did?

EVA. The police, you know, SS officers, they came to the house and my father answered the door in his dressing gown.

And I remember very clearly, I was lying in bed with my mother and she put her finger to her lips and she told me to climb under the bed. And I thought it was all terribly fun, we were going to be playing a trick on my father, *Versteckspiel*, so I did as she said and I got under the bed and I crawled as far back as I could and I waited.

SUSAN. And the reason for them coming to the house…

EVA. Something to do with the practice I think. He was still seeing patients and they said he'd broken some law or other, I didn't understand at the time.

SUSAN. And your mother, my grandmother

EVA. Well my mother wasn't Jewish.

SUSAN. No, I know.

EVA. Which was dreadful because I went to a Jewish school and they all made fun of me. But of course she was married to my father and so they took her as well.

SUSAN. But she got out, didn't she.

EVA. Yes, they released her eventually. She had a friend you see, a lawyer, and he somehow managed to convince them all that my mother and father were in the process of getting a divorce.

SUSAN. Were they?

EVA. Not at all, but when they asked my father if it was true he said yes, and so they signed the papers and that was that.

SUSAN. And you?

EVA. Well I waited under the bed, and when I finally came out they were both gone.

SUSAN. And so

> was that when you went to live with your grandparents?

EVA. That's right, with my *Omi und Opa*, my non-Jewish grandparents. *Essener Straße*. The house with the blue door. I adored that house. You could see the park from my bedroom window.

> Anyway, they put me in a new school and on the first day of term the teacher gave out free brown jackets to all the children. And of course my grandparents thought it was a good idea if I wore the jacket because then nobody would think I was half-Jewish or anything like that.

> So I had this brown jacket and I became a member of the Hitler Youth.

SUSAN. Right.

EVA. It seems odd when one thinks about it now. But it was great fun, we did all sorts of things together, went on outings and hikes, sang songs...

SUSAN. What sort of songs?

EVA. Well, we sang a lot about Hitler.

> (*Singing.*)
> *Wir marschieren für Hitler durch Nacht und durch Not*
> *Mit der Fahne der Jugend für Freiheit und Brot*

> Forever talking about death. '*Ja die Fahne ist mehr als der Tod.*'

SUSAN. What does that mean?

EVA. 'Yes the flag is more than death.'

> We had other songs too. I was asking a German recently whether they knew any of these songs but they didn't. I suppose they're not very fashionable.

SUSAN. But surely

> I mean your father was in prison

> I mean weren't you aware of the situation?

EVA. Well no. I was nine. Rosie's age.

SUSAN. So at what point did you realise that Germany wasn't a safe place for you?

EVA. I didn't. One day my grandmother took me shopping for a raincoat because she said it rained a lot in England and that was all I knew.

I did hear my grandfather say to her 'she won't be our responsibility any more', and I wondered what that meant.

What I can't understand to this day is why I wasn't terribly upset. I mean can you imagine? To be cut off like that from everything you know? I mean you'd think I'd be upset, wouldn't you?

Silence.

So I spent one last Christmas in Berlin and my grandmother taught me how to make marzipan.

SUSAN. And that's when you came to England.

EVA. That's right. For some reason I thought I was going to live with my mother. You know, she'd got out of prison and I thought we were leaving on the boat together. But she decided to stay and by the time she came to find me it was

well she was

She seemed like a foreigner.

We never really

understood each other

after that.

Mrs Lyons was awfully strict but she was ever so good to me and my foster brothers. She sent me to a Catholic school and of course none of the nuns spoke any German so I had to learn English.

SUSAN. Did you keep in touch with your friends from Berlin?

EVA. No. I mean I did write. But they didn't write back.

I remember there was one lesson in which the teacher asked everyone to describe their father's profession. And I said that mine was in a concentration camp. But I don't think they believed it. In any case, they didn't know what that meant.

SUSAN. And did you write letters to him?

EVA. Yes. He asked for letters. I've got the letters he wrote to my mother, they're here somewhere. He was allowed to write at the beginning, that's how we knew where they'd taken him.

I suppose what kept him alive for so long was the thought that he'd remarry my mother. But who knows.

He would've got out if he hadn't

He was a doctor you see. Doctors had privileges.

SUSAN. When did you hear?

EVA. I was fifteen. It was the hottest day of the year and we were having a picnic in the garden. Corned-beef sandwiches and lemonade.

He'd been in various prisons and camps. Germany, Poland, they were forever moving him around.

SUSAN. Who told you?

EVA. Some official. A Red Cross person or

They told me he was shot whilst trying to escape and

SUSAN. …

And?

EVA. and whether or not that's true, I

I don't know.

I didn't really know what to do with it.

I didn't really react to it.

Silence.

What are you going to do with *this*?

EVA *taps the tape recorder.*

SUSAN. Careful, I

I don't know, I

EVA. I mean what's the point.

SUSAN. I told you, it's something to

EVA. They're just stories. There'll come a point when nobody can remember. Sooner or later they'll all bleed into one another and

SUSAN. But I want to. Remember.

EVA. Why?

SUSAN. Because it's

I don't know, it's

Something.

Instead of nothing.

Because sometimes I think that perhaps it would have been better, made sense, been easier for me if

EVA. Easier for *you*?

SUSAN. if I'd you know, had something. To believe in. A religion or something. A faith.

EVA. You had Christmas and Easter. Still do.

SUSAN. Yes, I suppose.

Silence.

EVA. You'd better go.

SUSAN. But we haven't finished yet.

EVA. He'll be back soon.

SUSAN. Mum.

EVA. He doesn't like it.

SUSAN. Doesn't like what.

EVA. He'll sulk.

SUSAN. I wish we didn't have to do it like this.

I shouldn't need to ask his permission to see my own mother for God's sake.

EVA. He's a bore.

SUSAN. And now that you've actually got some time, now that you're not working and we could actually

EVA. A big fat bore.

SUSAN. I mean we could have lunch sometimes. Couldn't we? Just the two of us. He doesn't have to *be there* all the time, watching over you.

EVA. Oh don't be silly.

SUSAN. I'm not being silly, he's *been there* since I was eighteen years old and this has nothing to do with him.

EVA. Well yes. That's the problem.

They don't talk about it. Men. It's as if they're all sworn to secrecy.

SUSAN. Why? What happened to him?

EVA. You know what happened to him, he had a ghastly time.

SUSAN. I know he came on the Kindertransport, that's it.

EVA. Lost all of them.

SUSAN. You mean his family?

EVA. Looked for them but there's no record.

SUSAN. Why won't he

I mean it might help to

EVA. He had a ghastly time and he wants to forget about it.

Everybody told us to forget about it. Now we're all dying and everybody wants us to remember.

SUSAN. You're not dying. Not yet.

EVA. Harry never talked about it either.

SUSAN. No. I know.

EVA. You look so much like him.

SUSAN. Dad. Yeah.

EVA. Sometimes I have to remind myself that I ever gave birth to you.

SUSAN. But... but I am yours, Mum.

Silence.

EVA. I've got a present for Rosie.

SUSAN. ...

EVA. A chocolate rabbit.

SUSAN. Oh. Thank you. She'll like that.

EVA. Is she all right?

SUSAN. Yes. Well. She's been very quiet since Paul moved in but

but he's a good father to her. And I love him.

EVA. Do you?

SUSAN. Yes, really, I do.

EVA looks away.

EVA. I don't love Arnold.

SUSAN. Then what are you doing?

EVA. I've never loved Arnold.

SUSAN. There must have been something

EVA. Nothing.

SUSAN. Well then I really don't know what you're doing.

EVA. I've never loved a single hair on his body.

Click as the tape comes to the end of its side.

SUSAN *opens the tape recorder, takes the tape and places it in its case. Takes a pen and writes 'Mum 2002' on the front.*

The truth is I've never loved anyone.

SUSAN *puts down the tape and looks up at* EVA.

Any one or any thing. I don't know what it feels like. I suppose I'm too old to learn to feel it now.

I've said it hundreds of times, onstage and off. But I've never

you know

felt it.

SUSAN. Mum.

EVA. Not even you.

I didn't feel love when you were growing inside me. Didn't feel love when the pain started. Didn't feel love when I pushed you out.

I felt something, I'm sure. But it wasn't love.

Silence.

SUSAN. I don't believe you.

You're lying.

EVA. I'm not.

SUSAN. You love me very much.

EVA. Oh stop it.

SUSAN. You've always loved me.

EVA. This isn't about *you*, Susan.

SUSAN. Just because you can't say it, doesn't mean

EVA. You came to hear my story.

SUSAN. Yes. I know.

EVA. Well there it is.

SUSAN. But we haven't

EVA. Something to remember.

SUSAN. We haven't finished.

Blackout.

Six

2015

…or perhaps the scene changes around them. The garden of a private nursing home in Hertfordshire or somewhere like that.

It's spring and the flowers are starting to bud. EVA *and* SUSAN *sit as before, without the tape recorder.*

SUSAN. The nurse said you're having a good day.

EVA. She did, did she.

SUSAN. Have you eaten anything?

EVA. Ask Arnold.

SUSAN. You should try to finish your meals.

EVA. Arnold makes my meals.

SUSAN. Mum.

EVA. Arnold looks after me.

SUSAN. Arnold isn't here any more.

EVA. He's hiding in the bushes.

SUSAN. …

EVA. He doesn't want to see you.

SUSAN. Right.

EVA. I expect they'll find him sooner or later.

SUSAN. Who will?

EVA. They've been digging up the flowers.

SUSAN. The flowers look lovely.

EVA. Digging them all up and now they're coming for the bushes with the shears. Chopping them all down.

SUSAN. Well. They've got to maintain the garden, haven't they.

EVA. First the flowers, now the bushes.

SUSAN. Otherwise it'll get overgrown.

EVA. I know what they're doing.

SUSAN. They're keeping it nice for you.

EVA. They think I'm stupid but I know what's going on.

SUSAN. Nobody thinks you're stupid, Mum.

EVA. *They* do.

SUSAN. Who's they.

EVA. The men who call themselves the gardeners.

Silence.

I'd better get Arnold.

SUSAN. Arnold isn't

EVA. I'd better get him or they'll chop into him too.

SUSAN. Mum, please.

EVA. He knows where everything is you see.

SUSAN. We went to his funeral, remember?

EVA *gets up.*

They read a poem.

Remember?

Squints as though trying to see something in the bushes.

EVA. Arnold?

SUSAN. *I can still see you: an echo*

EVA. Are you there?

SUSAN. *that can be groped towards with antenna*

EVA. Arnold?

SUSAN. *words, on the ridge of parting.*

> *On recognising the poem,* EVA *launches into a theatrical recital:*

EVA. *Your face quietly shies*
when suddenly
there is lamplike brightness
inside me, just at the point
where most painfully one says, never.

SUSAN. There. You do remember.

EVA. Well of course I do, it's his favourite poem.

ARNOLD. CAN YOU HEAR THE POEM.

She looks again, but instead of ARNOLD *sees* ROSIE.

Oh it's you. There you are.

> ROSIE *enters. She rushes to* EVA *and hugs her.* EVA *sits back down.*

ROSIE. Sorry I'm late. We had a problem with the case. Well actually it was Sebastian's fault, he wanted to bring schnapps for you all but he didn't put it in the middle of the clothes like I told him to and now the bottle's cracked and it's leaked all over our clothes, just like I told him it would.

SUSAN. Oh dear.

ROSIE. So he's in the car park with Paul trying to get the broken glass out.

EVA. *Gebrochen.*

ROSIE. *Gebrochen, ja.*

> (*To* SUSAN.) So I'm sorry but when we get to yours we're going to have to put the whole lot in the washing machine and there won't be any schnapps.

SUSAN. Never mind.

ROSIE. Anyway.

SUSAN. It's nice to see you.

ROSIE. Yeah.

SUSAN. In person I mean.

ROSIE. …

How are you, Grandma?

EVA. I'm all right.

ROSIE. Good.

EVA. But what about you?

ROSIE. Yeah, no, good, I'm fine.

EVA. Are you?

ROSIE. No, absolutely fine, other than the schnapps incident.

EVA. You look different.

ROSIE. Do I?

EVA. Older. Younger. Thinner. Something.

ROSIE. Oh. Well.

EVA. When am I going to have a granddaughter?

SUSAN. You've got one, Mum, she's standing right there. Came all the way from Berlin to visit you.

EVA. Or a grandson. But I think I'd prefer a granddaughter. Someone to buy dresses for.

SUSAN. You mean great-granddaughter.

EVA. When are you having a baby?

ROSIE. Me?

EVA. I want a granddaughter, Susie.

ROSIE. Rosie.

SUSAN. That's Rosie, Mum.

EVA. I told you, didn't I, they're cutting down the roses.

SUSAN. *I'm* Susie.

EVA. Digging up the flowers.

ROSIE. I know you were worried about the flowers but I think you're right. I think they're helping them.

EVA. Oh you do, do you.

ROSIE. To grow. You know. You have to do that with flowers, don't you. Dig up the earth. Or something.

SUSAN. Yes, something like that.

ROSIE. Arnold liked gardening, didn't he.

SUSAN. Don't.

EVA. Arnold is hiding in the bushes.

ROSIE. Oh God.

SUSAN. The nurse said she was having a good day but

EVA. Nurse nurse nurse, will you shut up about the nurse.

SUSAN. …

ROSIE *inhales, as if about to speak.*

PAUL *and* SEBASTIAN *enter.*

PAUL. Sorry, sorry, minor emergency involving a bottle of schnapps.

SUSAN. Yes, we heard all about it.

SEBASTIAN. My fault. Hello.

SEBASTIAN *kisses* SUSAN *on the cheek.*

Rosie told me to put it in the middle of the clothes and I didn't.

PAUL. Panic over though.

SUSAN (*to* PAUL). God, you stink of alcohol.

ROSIE. Grandma, this is my boyfriend. Sebastian.

SEBASTIAN. It's good to meet you.

SEBASTIAN *holds out his hand*. EVA *stares at him hard*.

ROSIE. Grandma?

SEBASTIAN. Uh… Rosie speaks about you often.

ROSIE. Sebastian and I live together. In Berlin.

EVA. I know what Berlin is.

ROSIE. Yeah. I just

EVA. I used to live in Berlin.

ROSIE. Yeah I know. And now *I* do.

SEBASTIAN. *Rosie hat gesagt, Sie haben in der Essener Straße gelebt, in einem Haus mit blauer Tür.* [Rosie says you lived on Essener Strasse in a house with a blue door.]

EVA *clams up*.

EVA. No.

ROSIE. No what?

SUSAN. What did you say to her?

SEBASTIAN. I said about the house on *Essener Straße*, I

EVA. No.

SUSAN. Yes that's right, the house with the

EVA. Get him away from me.

SUSAN. Mum it's fine, he's

EVA. GET HIM AWAY.

EVA *gets to her feet and starts feebly attacking* SEBASTIAN *with her fists*.

Sie ist nicht mehr blau. [It isn't blue any more.]

ROSIE. GRANDMA.

EVA. *Sie ist* nicht *mehr blau.*

SUSAN. Mum, stop

STOP IT.

EVA. *Ich kann ohne Brille seh'n.* [I can see without glasses.]

SUSAN *tries to hold her while* SEBASTIAN *backs off.*

SUSAN. What's the matter with you? Honestly.

EVA. *Ich kann* ohne Brille seh'n.

EVA *keeps staring at him. Doesn't take her eyes off him.*

SUSAN. I'm so sorry. She isn't usually…

SEBASTIAN. No, it's

PAUL. Come on, Sebastian, why don't we take a walk.

SEBASTIAN. …

Yeah, no, sure.

PAUL. I'll show you the grounds. Spectacular grounds.

They start walking.

Costs a fortune but the grounds are spectacular.

…and exit.

EVA *goes back to her seat.*

EVA. It isn't blue any more.

ROSIE *pulls* SUSAN *to one side.*

ROSIE. Why did she do that?

SUSAN. I don't know. Sometimes it's… unpredictable.

ROSIE. He was only trying to be friendly.

SUSAN. It's probably because he's a new face. Or he reminds her of someone or

I don't know. He shouldn't take it personally.

ROSIE. *I'm* taking it personally.

SUSAN. Well you shouldn't.

ROSIE. I can't talk to her when she's like this.

SUSAN. You have to.

ROSIE. I don't know what to say.

SUSAN. The nurse said it's important to keep talking. Keep reminding her of things.

ROSIE. I don't know where to start.

SUSAN. Look I'm sorry but this stuff it's just

It's here.

ROSIE. Stuff.

SUSAN. It's complicated.

ROSIE. Well I don't need any more *stuff*. I'm full up already, I don't have room for it.

SUSAN. But it's here.

ROSIE. Yeah. In my blood. Right?

SUSAN. This isn't about you, Rosie.

ROSIE. Isn't it?

They stare at each other for a moment.

ROSIE *turns to* EVA.

I finished my degree, Grandma. Handed in my dissertation last week.

EVA. Aren't you clever.

ROSIE. I'm predicted a two-one.

EVA. When are you coming to see me?

ROSIE. I'm seeing you now.

EVA. You never come to see me.

ROSIE. I…

It's a long way.

EVA. Never call.

ROSIE. It's expensive.

EVA. Do you need some money?

ROSIE. No I didn't mean

No I'm fine.

EVA. Did I send you a cheque?

ROSIE. No but it's all right.

EVA. What would you like?

ROSIE. My birthday was in November.

EVA. Where's my chequebook?

SUSAN. It's probably inside.

EVA. How much do you need?

ROSIE. I don't need anything, I'm fine.

EVA. Ask Arnold. He knows where everything is.

ROSIE. ...

SUSAN. Okay, Mum. We'll do that.

ROSIE. Right.

Yes.

We'll do that.

Silence.

ROSIE *looks at* EVA. SUSAN *looks at* ROSIE. EVA *gazes into the distance.*

ROSIE *gets out her phone.*

SUSAN. What are you doing?

ROSIE. I want to take a photo.

SUSAN. Oh. Okay.

ROSIE. Why don't you

SUSAN. Shall I

SUSAN *stands beside* EVA.

ROSIE. Yeah.

Poses for a photo.

Well go on. Smile.

SUSAN attempts a smile. ROSIE taps the screen, then looks.

Quite good actually.

SUSAN looks.

SUSAN. Oh it's not, I look like a horse.

ROSIE. Grandma? What d'you think?

ROSIE shows EVA the photo.

No answer.

I'll get it printed if you like. When I go home.

Grandma?

…but she's far away.

EVA (*singing, quietly*).
*Nun ade du mein lieb Heimatland
Lieb Heimatland ade…*

She continues to sing or hum throughout the next few lines.

ROSIE. What's she…

SUSAN. It's a German folk song.

ROSIE. I haven't heard it before.

SUSAN. She used to sing it sometimes.

ROSIE. *Heimat.*

SUSAN. Home.

ROSIE. Yeah. But in German the word holds a different meaning.

SUSAN. Well. I thought it meant home.

ROSIE. Untranslatable. Apparently.

Blackout.

End.

A Nick Hern Book

Now This Is Not The End first published in Great Britain as a paperback original in 2015 by Nick Hern Books Limited, The Glasshouse, 49a Goldhawk Road, London W12 8QP, in association with Rebecca Targett Productions and Raising Silver Theatre

Now This Is Not The End copyright © 2015 Rose Lewenstein

Rose Lewenstein has asserted her right to be identified as the author of this work

Cover image: Rebecca Pitt

Designed and typeset by Nick Hern Books, London
Printed in the UK by Mimeo Ltd, Huntingdon, Cambridgeshire PE29 6XX

A CIP catalogue record for this book is available from the British Library

ISBN 978 1 84842 460 9

CAUTION All rights whatsoever in this play are strictly reserved. Requests to reproduce the text in whole or in part should be addressed to the publisher.

Amateur Performing Rights Applications for performance, including readings and excerpts, by amateurs in the English language throughout the world should be addressed to the Performing Rights Manager, Nick Hern Books, The Glasshouse, 49a Goldhawk Road, London W12 8QP, *tel* +44 (0)20 8749 4953, *email* rights@nickhernbooks.co.uk, except as follows:

Australia: Dominie Drama, 8 Cross Street, Brookvale 2100, *tel* (2) 9938 8686 *fax* (2) 9938 8695, *email* drama@dominie.com.au

New Zealand: Play Bureau, PO Box 9013, St Clair, Dunedin 9047, *tel* (3) 455 9959, *email* info@playbureau.com

South Africa: DALRO (pty) Ltd, PO Box 31627, 2017 Braamfontein, *tel* (11) 712 8000, *fax* (11) 403 9094, *email* theatricals@dalro.co.za

United States and Canada: Troika, as below

Professional Performing Rights Applications for performance by professionals in any medium and in any language throughout the world (and by amateur and stock companies in the United States of America and Canada) should be addressed to Troika, 10a Christina Street, London, EC2A 4PA, *tel* +44 (0)20 7336 7868, *web* www.troikatalent.com

No performance of any kind may be given unless a licence has been obtained. Applications should be made before rehearsals begin. Publication of this play does not necessarily indicate its availability for performance.

www.nickhernbooks.co.uk

facebook.com/nickhernbooks

twitter.com/nickhernbooks